Making History: The Obamas

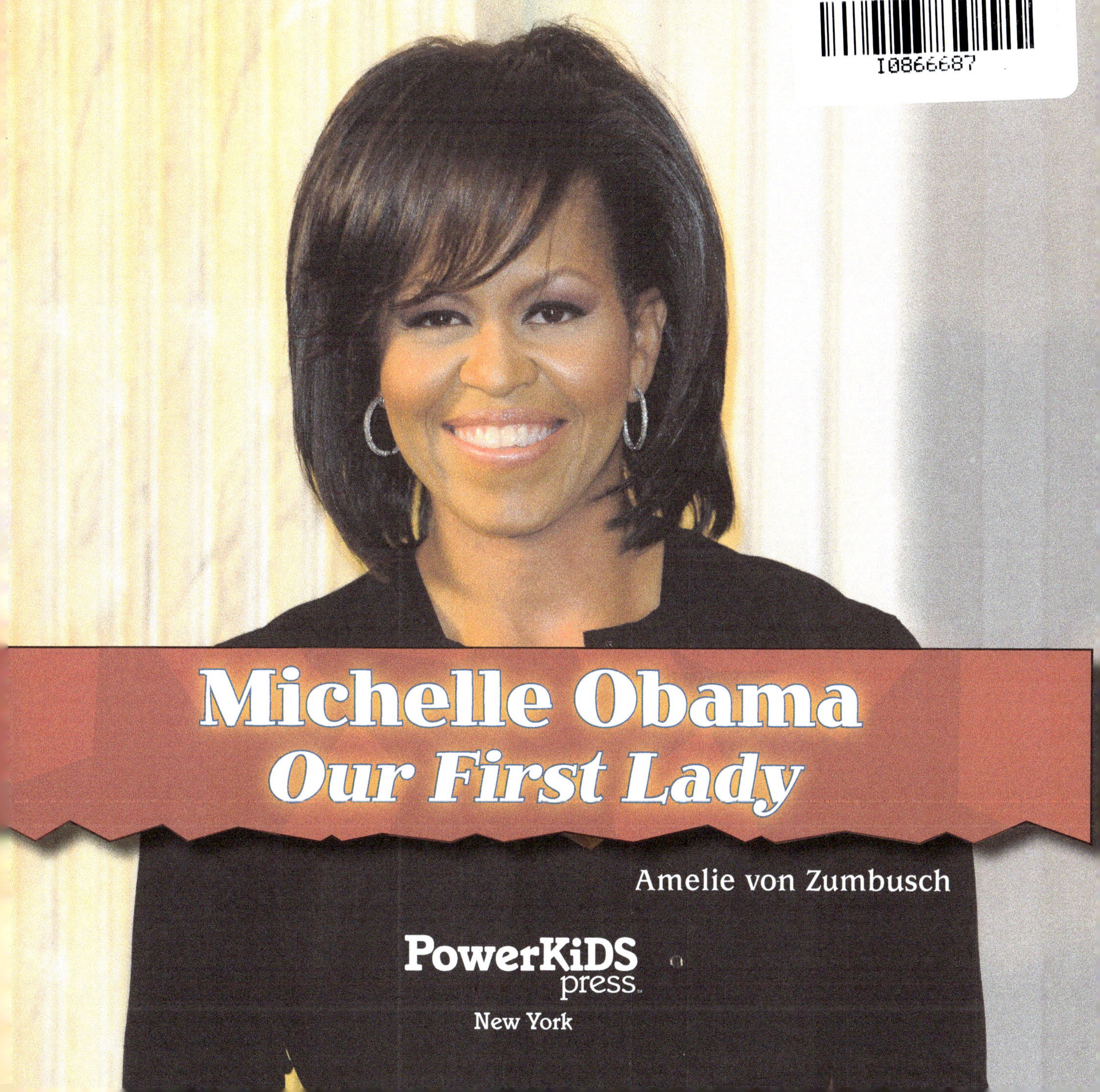

Michelle Obama
Our First Lady

Amelie von Zumbusch

PowerKiDS press
New York

Published in 2010 by The Rosen Publishing Group, Inc.
29 East 21st Street, New York, NY 10010

First Edition

Editors: Nicole Pristash and Maggie Murphy
Book Design: Kate Laczynski
Photo Researcher: Jessica Gerweck

Photo Credits: Cover Pascal Le Segretain/Getty Images; p. 4 Dmitry Kostyukov/AFP/Getty Images; p. 6 © AP Photo/Ron Edmonds; p. 6 (inset) Saul Loeb/AFP/Getty Images; p. 8 © www.iStockphoto.com/Almin Tang; p. 8 (inset) © Rapport/Newscom; p. 10 Mandel Ngan/AFP/Getty Images; p. 12 Scott Olson/Getty Images; p. 14 Ethan Miller/Getty Images; p. 16 Paul J. Richards/AFP/Getty Images; p. 18 Jewel Samad/AFP/Getty Images; p. 20 Paul Morigi/Getty Images for Sunshine Sachs and Associates.

Library of Congress Cataloging-in-Publication Data

Zumbusch, Amelie von.
Michelle Obama : our First Lady / Amelie von Zumbusch. — 1st ed.
p. cm. — (Making history: the Obamas)
Includes index.
ISBN 978-1-4358-9388-7 (library binding) — ISBN 978-1-4358-9868-4 (pbk.) — ISBN 978-1-4358-9869-1 (6-pack)
1. Obama, Michelle, 1964—Juvenile literature. 2. Presidents' spouses—United States—Biography—Juvenile literature. 3. Legislators' spouses—United States—Biography—Juvenile literature. 4. African American women lawyers—Illinois—Chicago—Biography—Juvenile literature. 5. Chicago (Ill.)—Biography—Juvenile literature I. Title.
E909.O24Z86 2010
973.932092—dc22
[B] 2009034253

Manufactured in the United States of America

CPSIA Compliance Information: Batch #WW10PK: For Further Information contact Rosen Publishing, New York, New York at 1-800-237-9932

Contents

Meet Michelle Obama 5
Her Family Life 7
Smart and Hardworking 9
Meeting Barack 11
A Happy Time 13
On the Campaign Trail 15
The New First Lady 17
Down-to-Earth 19
Someone to Look Up To 21
The Years to Come 22
Glossary 23
Index 24
Web Sites 24

Meet Michelle Obama

People across the United States pay close attention to what the First Lady does. After all, the First Lady is the wife of the president of the United States. Over the years, there have been many First Ladies. However, Michelle Obama is the very first African-American First Lady.

African Americans were treated badly throughout much of American history. Until 1865, many African Americans were **slaves**. In fact, some of Michelle Obama's **ancestors** were slaves. The fact that she is now the First Lady shows how far this country has come. Today, people of all races look up to this smart, hardworking woman.

People all over the world are excited to meet the First Lady of the United States, Michelle Obama. Here, she is shown visiting schoolchildren in Russia.

Her Family Life

Before she married Barack Obama, Michelle Obama's name was Michelle Robinson. Michelle was born to Fraser and Marian Robinson on January 17, 1964. Michelle grew up with her mother, father, and her older brother, Craig, on the South Side of Chicago, Illinois.

Fraser and Marian did all that they could to make sure that their kids lived up to their dreams. When the children were young, Marian stayed home to care for them. She taught both children to read by the time they were four years old! Even though Fraser had **multiple sclerosis**, he worked long hours to **support** his family.

Here, Michelle and her brother Craig (right) stand together with Michelle's daughter Sasha (center) in 2008. *Inset:* Michelle's mother, Marian Robinson.

Smart and Hardworking

Michelle's older brother, Craig, was a good student. After high school, he went to Princeton University, in New Jersey. Michelle wanted to prove herself as smart as her big brother, so she worked hard. In 1981, Michelle also started studying at Princeton. She studied sociology, or the study of how communities work. Michelle took classes in African-American studies, as well. She wrote a long paper about African Americans who had gone to Princeton.

After Princeton, Michelle went to law school at Harvard University, in Cambridge, Massachusetts. When she finished law school in 1988, Michelle moved back to Chicago to work as a **lawyer**.

Working hard at Princeton University, shown here, helped Michelle succeed in life. *Inset:* Michelle in her Princeton graduation photo, from 1985.

Meeting Barack

In Chicago, Michelle worked for a big law firm. In 1989, she met a law-school student who was working there for the summer. His name was Barack Obama. Obama liked Michelle right away, but she was not so sure that she liked him. Obama then asked her to come with him to a community meeting. Michelle watched Obama talk to people from a poor part of Chicago. Michelle liked how much he wanted to help them. Soon, the pair started dating. In 1992, they got married.

Barack calls Michelle his rock. This means that he depends on her. Barack knows that he can always count on Michelle to tell him the truth.

As First Lady, Michelle attends important events with her husband. Here they are shown after having dinner with U.S. governors in February 2009.

A Happy Time

Michelle had a good job as a lawyer, but she wanted to help others even more. Shortly before her marriage, Michelle left the law firm where she had been working and started working for the mayor of Chicago instead. She went on to work for another city office and a group that trained young people to be leaders in their communities. Later, Michelle worked for the University of Chicago.

Michelle was happy to be making a difference in the city she called home. The birth of her daughters, Malia, in 1998, and Sasha, in 2001, also brought her great joy.

Here, Michelle and Barack spend time with Sasha (left) and Malia (right) on the night Barack was elected to the U.S. Senate, November 4, 2004.

CHANGE
WE NEED
WWW.BARACKOBAMA.COM
CHANGE
WE CAN
BELIEVE IN

On the Campaign Trail

In 2004, Barack Obama was **elected** to the U.S. **Senate**. He spent part of his time in Washington, but Michelle generally stayed in Chicago to work and care for her daughters. In 2007, Obama announced that he would run for president. Michelle decided to leave her job so that she could **campaign** with him.

Michelle spoke to big crowds about why her husband would make a good president. She said, "Millions of Americans know that Barack understands their dreams; that Barack will fight for people like them." Many voters agreed with Michelle, and Obama was elected president on November 4, 2008.

Michelle campaigned for her husband in many different U.S. cities. Here she is shown speaking at a rally in Las Vegas, Nevada, in October 2008.

Class Rules
Thank you

The New First Lady

On January 20, 2009, Barack Obama became president of the United States. The Obama family then moved into the White House, a big house in Washington, D.C., in which the U.S. president lives. The first thing Michelle dealt with was getting Malia and Sasha settled into their new home and their new school. Michelle's mother moved into the White House, too, so that she could help care for the girls.

Michelle decided to use her new job to support causes in which she believes. She supports working mothers and military families. Michelle is also pushing for all Americans to **volunteer** in their communities.

Supporting military families is important to Michelle. Here, she is shown visiting children at Fort Bragg, a military base in North Carolina.

BANCROFT

Down-To-Earth

Michelle Obama is known for saying what is on her mind. She has an open, easy way of talking to people. While her husband speaks movingly about big ideas, Michelle is generally more **practical**. She tries hard to stay down-to-earth and to make sure that her daughters have fairly normal lives.

In her free time, Michelle likes watching old TV shows. She is a big fan of exercising, too. Michelle has been known to get up very early to work out. She is also interested in fresh, healthy food. In fact, Michelle helped plant a vegetable garden at the White House!

Here you can see Michelle working with a group of fifth-grade students in the garden that she helped plant at the White House.

Someone to Look Up To

Now that she is the First Lady, reporters follow everything that Michelle Obama does. One of the things that has caught many people's attention is her sense of style. Michelle often wears clothes that are made by new, young **designers**. People across the country look up to and copy her style.

However, Michelle's style is not the biggest reason why people look up to her. People like that she is a smart, successful woman and a good mother. Michelle's story proves that you can go far if you work hard. Her story offers hope to both women and African Americans.

People look up to Michelle because she makes time to help others. Here, she is shown volunteering at a food bank in Washington, D.C., in April 2009.

The Years to Come

Now that Washington, D.C., is her home, Michelle Obama is getting to know the city. She wants to help make a difference there. Michelle has already visited many schools, and she has met with people to talk about how to improve Washington's and the country's school system.

Michelle will make official visits to countries around the world, too. During the summer of 2009, she brought Malia and Sasha along to visit Europe and Africa. Raising her daughters well continues to be the most important thing to her. She wants them to be good **citizens**. As Michelle said, "Each of us has something to **contribute** to the life of this nation."

Glossary

ancestors (AN-ses-terz) Relatives who lived long ago.

campaign (kam-PAYN) To work for a certain result, such as winning an election.

citizens (SIH-tih-zenz) People who were born in or have a right to live in a country or other community.

contribute (kon-trih-BYOOT) To give.

designers (dih-ZY-nurz) People who make clothes.

elected (ee-LEK-tid) Picked for an office by voters.

lawyer (LAH-yer) A person who gives advice about the law and who speaks for people in court.

multiple sclerosis (MUL-tuh-pel skleh-ROH-sus) A sickness that hurts the nervous system.

practical (PRAK-tih-kul) Interested in real-world answers to problems.

Senate (SEH-nit) A law-making part of the U.S. government.

slaves (SLAYVZ) People who are "owned" by other people and forced to work for no pay.

support (suh-PORT) To give money or necessities.

volunteer (vah-lun-TEER) To give one's time without pay.

Index

A
African Americans, 5, 9
ancestors, 5

C
citizens, 22

D
designers, 21

J
job, 13, 15, 17

L
lawyer, 9, 13

M
multiple sclerosis, 7

O
Obama, Barack (husband), 7, 11, 15, 17, 19
Obama, Malia (daughter), 13, 15, 17, 19, 22
Obama, Sasha (daughter), 13, 15, 17, 19, 22

P
president, 5, 15, 17

R
Robinson, Fraser (father), 7
Robinson, Marian (mother), 7, 17

S
Senate, 15
slaves, 5

U
United States, 5, 17

V
voters, 15

Web Sites

Due to the changing nature of Internet links, PowerKids Press has developed an online list of Web sites related to the subject of this book. This site is updated regularly. Please use this link to access the list:
www.powerkidslinks.com/obamas/mich/